DATE DUE			

33107435

362.29
SAN

Sanders, Pete.

Drinking alcohol

**MEADOW'S EDGE ELEMENTARY
MISHAWAKA INDIANA**

WHAT DO YOU KNOW ABOUT

ADRINKING LCOHOL

PETE SANDERS and STEVE MYERS

COPPER BEECH BOOKS

BROOKFIELD, CONNECTICUT

Designed and produced by
Aladdin Books Ltd
28 Percy Street
London W1P OLD

First published in the United States
in 1997 by Copper Beech Books,
an imprint of
The Millbrook Press
2 Old New Milford Road
Brookfield, Connecticut 06804

Printed in Belgium

Design   David West
                Children's
                Book Design
Editor   Sarah Levete
Picture research Brooks Krikler
                Research
Illustrators   Mike Lacey
                Ian Thompson

Library of Congress Cataloging-in-
Publication Data

Sanders, Pete.
Drinking alcohol / Pete Sanders and
Steve Myers.
     p. cm. — (What do you know
about)
Includes index.
Summary: Discusses what alcohol is,
why people drink it, and how it can
affect people's health and well-being.
ISBN 0-7613-0573-4
1. Alcoholism—Juvenile literature.
2. Drinking of alcoholic beverages—
Juvenile literature. [1. Alcohol.
2. Alcoholism.] I. Myers, Steve. II. Title.
III. Series: Sanders, Pete. What do you
know about.
HV5066.S34 1997   96-35823
362.29'2—dc20   CIP AC

CONTENTS

HOW TO USE THIS BOOK

The books in this series are intended to help young people to understand more about issues that may affect their lives.

Each book can be read by a young person alone, or together with a parent, teacher, or helper. Issues raised in the storyline are further discussed in the accompanying text, so that there is an opportunity to talk through ideas as they come up.

At the end of the book there is a section called "What Can We Do?" This gives practical ideas which will be useful for both young people and adults. Organizations and helplines are also listed, to provide the reader with additional sources of information and support.

INTRODUCTION

DRINKING ALCOHOL IS A PART OF MANY PEOPLE'S SOCIAL LIVES. IT IS OFTEN ASSOCIATED WITH HAVING A GOOD TIME.

However, alcohol is a drug. It can have a damaging effect on the body and may influence the way in which people behave. Like most drugs, it can cause emotional and physical problems if it is not used sensibly.

This book will help you to have a better knowledge of alcohol, why people drink it, and how it can affect people's health and well-being. Each chapter introduces a different aspect of the subject, illustrated by a continuing storyline. The characters in the story are involved in situations which many people may face in their lives. After each episode, we stop and consider the issues raised, and broaden the discussion. By the end of the book, you will understand more about alcohol and the way that it can affect people's lives.

I THOUGHT IT WOULD MAKE ME FEEL MORE CONFIDENT BUT I JUST FEEL OUT OF CONTROL.

THAT'S WHAT DAD SAID. I REMEMBER WHEN HE AND MOM ARGUED, HE SAID TERRIBLE THINGS. I KNOW HE DIDN'T MEAN THEM, BUT HE STILL SAID THEM.

YOU NEED TO GET SOME HELP, SCOTT. PLEASE TALK TO MOM AND DAD.

ALCOHOLIC DRINKS

ALCOHOL HAS BEEN DRUNK IN DIFFERENT FORMS FOR MANY CENTURIES.

Today, drinking alcohol is accepted in most societies, and there is a wide range of alcoholic drinks available.

The scientific name for the alcohol in a drink is ethanol. This is produced by sugar, water, and yeast combining together in a chemical process called fermentation. Different types of alcoholic drinks are made in a variety of ways and contain varying amounts of alcohol. Beer contains less alcohol than wine. It is produced from fermented grains, such as corn, barley, rye, or wheat. Wine is made by fermenting the juice of grapes or other fruits. Gin, whisky, vodka, brandy, and rum are distilled spirits. These are strong in alcohol and are made by heating fermented grains or wine. Sherry and port are a mix of wine with some spirit. They are known as fortified wines. Other ingredients may be added to change the flavor or color of all of these drinks. An alcoholic drink may not even taste of alcohol – there are an increasing number of so-called soft drinks to which alcohol has been added.

Alcohol is sometimes a symbol of hospitality and may be offered at meals or any special occasion along with soft drinks.

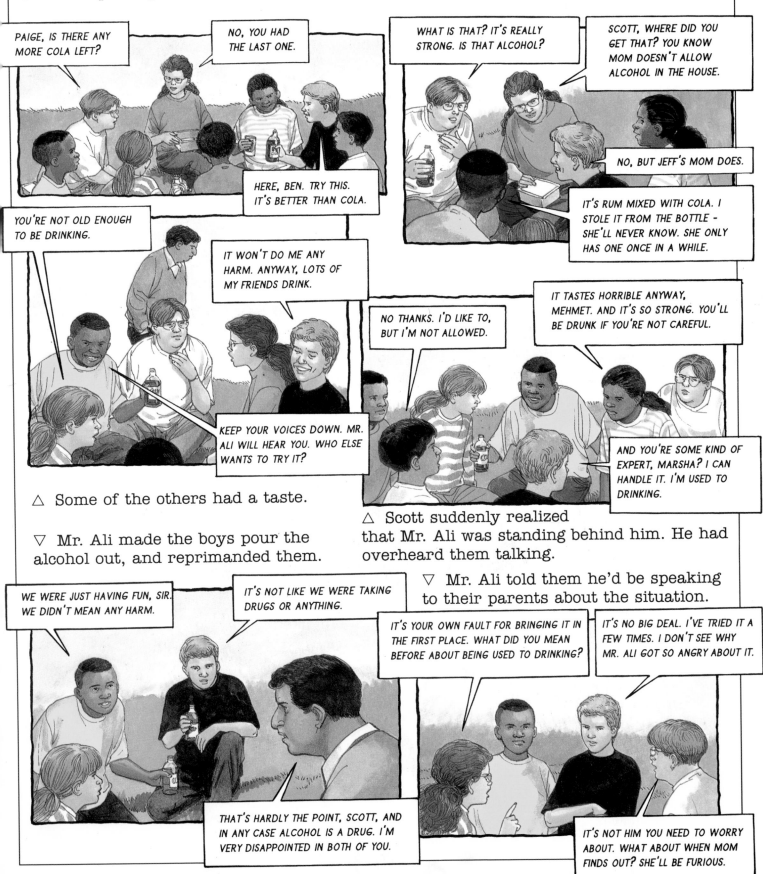

▽ Scott, Ben, and Paige Fisher were on a school trip. They had stopped for lunch.

PAIGE, IS THERE ANY MORE COLA LEFT?

NO, YOU HAD THE LAST ONE.

HERE, BEN. TRY THIS. IT'S BETTER THAN COLA.

YOU'RE NOT OLD ENOUGH TO BE DRINKING.

IT WON'T DO ME ANY HARM. ANYWAY, LOTS OF MY FRIENDS DRINK.

KEEP YOUR VOICES DOWN. MR. ALI WILL HEAR YOU. WHO ELSE WANTS TO TRY IT?

△ Some of the others had a taste.

▽ Mr. Ali made the boys pour the alcohol out, and reprimanded them.

WE WERE JUST HAVING FUN, SIR. WE DIDN'T MEAN ANY HARM.

IT'S NOT LIKE WE WERE TAKING DRUGS OR ANYTHING.

THAT'S HARDLY THE POINT, SCOTT, AND IN ANY CASE ALCOHOL IS A DRUG. I'M VERY DISAPPOINTED IN BOTH OF YOU.

▽ Ben took a drink, and began to cough.

WHAT IS THAT? IT'S REALLY STRONG. IS THAT ALCOHOL?

SCOTT, WHERE DID YOU GET THAT? YOU KNOW MOM DOESN'T ALLOW ALCOHOL IN THE HOUSE.

NO, BUT JEFF'S MOM DOES.

IT'S RUM MIXED WITH COLA. I STOLE IT FROM THE BOTTLE - SHE'LL NEVER KNOW. SHE ONLY HAS ONE ONCE IN A WHILE.

IT TASTES HORRIBLE ANYWAY, MEHMET. AND IT'S SO STRONG. YOU'LL BE DRUNK IF YOU'RE NOT CAREFUL.

NO THANKS. I'D LIKE TO, BUT I'M NOT ALLOWED.

AND YOU'RE SOME KIND OF EXPERT, MARSHA? I CAN HANDLE IT. I'M USED TO DRINKING.

△ Scott suddenly realized that Mr. Ali was standing behind him. He had overheard them talking.

▽ Mr. Ali told them he'd be speaking to their parents about the situation.

IT'S YOUR OWN FAULT FOR BRINGING IT IN THE FIRST PLACE. WHAT DID YOU MEAN BEFORE ABOUT BEING USED TO DRINKING?

IT'S NO BIG DEAL. I'VE TRIED IT A FEW TIMES. I DON'T SEE WHY MR. ALI GOT SO ANGRY ABOUT IT.

IT'S NOT HIM YOU NEED TO WORRY ABOUT. WHAT ABOUT WHEN MOM FINDS OUT? SHE'LL BE FURIOUS.

Ben and Marsha know that some drinks are much stronger in alcohol than others.
Even drinks which look or taste similar can vary in their alcoholic content. The strength of alcohol is usually measured by calculating the percentage of ethanol in any particular drink. The unit system is a guideline to a drink's alcoholic strength – for instance, a glass of wine, half a pint of beer, and a single measure of whisky are equal to one unit of alcohol. At home, drinks may not be poured to the exact measures used in clubs, bars, and restaurants so people may be drinking more "units" than they realize.

Mr. Ali has said that alcohol is a powerful drug.
However, many people do not always view alcohol in the same way as they do other drugs. This may be because alcohol is legally and freely available to adults in most countries. But alcohol drunk in large amounts can have a serious effect on your physical and emotional health. More people die each year from the effects of alcohol than from illegal drug abuse.

There are laws about the age at which people can buy alcohol in stores and drinks in clubs or bars.
However, there are few restrictions about drinking alcohol in the home or elsewhere, even for young people. Some people believe there should be tighter regulations concerning the consumption of alcohol, just as there are strict laws concerning the use and abuse of other drugs.

WHY DO PEOPLE DRINK ALCOHOL?

PEOPLE MAY CHOOSE TO DRINK ALCOHOL FOR A VARIETY OF REASONS.

Many people enjoy the taste of alcohol and the immediate effects they experience having had a drink.

Some say that alcohol helps them to unwind and relax. People who are shy sometimes believe that alcohol will help them to overcome their fears. Many feel obliged to drink because of the social situation they are in. Some people drink out of habit.

Alcohol is often available in the most popular meeting places for adults – bars, restaurants, and clubs. As a result, having a good time is often associated with alcohol being available. Because of this, it is easy for alcohol to become a part of a person's lifestyle. Drinking is seen as an "adult" thing to do. Advertisers are aware of this and will often make drinking alcohol look sophisticated and special. This can often have an influence on a person's decision to start drinking.

Young people may begin to drink alcohol in order to impress others or perhaps because others dare them to do so.

▽ It was two weeks later, near the end of the semester.

ALI'S SUCH A HYPOCRITE, GOING ON ABOUT HOW DRINKING'S BAD FOR YOU. I PASSED THE STAFF ROOM EARLIER. THEY'RE GIVING HIM A PARTY LATER - THERE'S LOADS OF BOOZE IN THERE.

I'M GLAD HE'S LEAVING THIS SEMESTER. MY DAD NEVER DRINKS ALCOHOL SO I GOT INTO REAL TROUBLE BECAUSE ALI TOLD HIM ABOUT WHAT HAPPENED ON THE SCHOOL TRIP.

BY THE WAY, JOHNNY CHRISTIAN INVITED ME TO A PARTY AT HIS HOUSE TONIGHT. DO YOU WANT TO COME? IT SHOULD BE GREAT.

I CAN'T. ANYWAY, I DIDN'T KNOW YOU KNEW JOHNNY. SINCE WHEN HAVE YOU BEEN HANGING AROUND WITH HIM?

NOT LONG. JOHNNY'S A LOT OF FUN. HE'S COOL. HE AND HIS GIRLFRIEND EVEN LOOK OLD ENOUGH TO GET INTO BARS. COME ALONG TONIGHT.

I'M IN ENOUGH TROUBLE. MOM AND DAD GROUNDED ME FOR A MONTH BUT AT LEAST THEY LET ME GO TO SWIM PRACTICE.

△ Johnny Christian was two years ahead of them in school.

▽ That evening, Ben and Paige went to Marsha's house. Their mothers worked for the same company, and the two families planned to go on vacation together.

I THOUGHT SCOTT WAS COMING TOO.

HE WAS GOING TO, BUT HE CHANGED HIS MIND. HE'S GONE OUT SHOPPING WITH HIS FRIENDS.

HE'S HARDLY EVER HERE THESE DAYS. I HOPE HE'S NOT GETTING INTO ANY TROUBLE.

△ Scott and Jeff were both trying out for the school swim team.

▽ At dinner, Marsha's sister Rachel and her husband Laurence had a surprise for the family.

▽ Mr. Sharpe fetched the champagne. He asked if Ben and Paige could have some too.

I SAW THE DOCTOR TODAY. I'M GOING TO HAVE A BABY.

DARLING, THAT'S WONDERFUL. I'M SO PLEASED.

CONGRATULATIONS!

THIS CALLS FOR A CELEBRATION. THERE'S SOME CHAMPAGNE IN THE FRIDGE. LET'S TOAST THE GOOD NEWS.

GO AHEAD, MOM. JUST A LITTLE.

OK. JUST THIS ONCE, BECAUSE IT'S A SPECIAL OCCASION. BUT JUST HALF A GLASS EACH.

CONGRATULATIONS!

CONGRATULATIONS!

▽ After dinner, Marsha, Ben, and Paige went up to Marsha's room.

I CAN'T BELIEVE MOM LET US HAVE A DRINK. SHE'S USUALLY SO STRICT ABOUT IT.

SHE'S STILL UPSET ABOUT DAD, THAT'S ALL.

DOES HE STILL DRINK?

▽ Mr. Fisher had begun to drink heavily after he lost his job and was unable to find new employment.

NO, HE SEEMS FINE NOW - AT LEAST HE IS ON THE WEEKENDS WHEN WE'VE SEEN HIM.

BEFORE, HE'D SAY THAT ALCOHOL HELPED HIM FORGET HIS PROBLEMS. BUT IT JUST MADE HIM MORE UNHAPPY.

▽ Paige said that her parents had begun to argue more and more.

▽ Marsha asked where Scott was.

THEY WENT ON LIKE THAT FOR MONTHS BEFORE THEY SPLIT UP. MOM BLAMED DAD'S DRINKING. SHE STOPPED HAVING ALCOHOL IN THE HOUSE. SHE WAS FURIOUS WITH SCOTT ABOUT THE SCHOOL TRIP.

HE'S AT A PARTY WITH JOHNNY CHRISTIAN. HONESTLY, THAT'S ALL HE EVER TALKS ABOUT NOW - HOW GREAT HIS NEW FRIEND IS.

HE'S OLDER, ISN'T HE? I'VE HEARD THE OTHERS TALKING ABOUT HIM - HE'S GOT A BAD REPUTATION, HE'S ALWAYS IN TROUBLE.

▽ Scott was late coming home that night. Ben and Paige heard him come in.

WHERE HAVE YOU BEEN? MOM'S FRANTIC. SHE'S ON THE PHONE TO JEFF'S HOUSE NOW, TRYING TO FIND OUT WHERE JOHNNY LIVES.

SO WHAT? IT WAS A GREAT PARTY. I COULDN'T CARE LESS WHAT TIME IT IS. TELL MOM I'VE GONE STRAIGHT TO BED.

BUT SHE'LL WANT TO TALK TO YOU. YOU CAN'T EXPECT US TO COVER FOR YOU, SCOTT.

△ Scott refused to listen and went upstairs.

SHE WAS ALL SET TO DRIVE OVER TO FIND YOU. WHAT'S THE MATTER, ANYWAY? YOU'VE BEEN DRINKING, HAVEN'T YOU?

Some people, like Jeff's dad, choose not to drink alcohol for a variety of reasons.

They may decide not to drink because they do not like the taste, or because they know it will affect their health. Or, they may have religious or cultural beliefs which forbid the use of alcohol. Alcohol affects people's abilities and judgments. Lots of people choose not to drink in certain situations where they need to remain clear-headed. Athletes often avoid alcohol because they know that it will impair their performance.

Paige and Ben's dad drank alcohol to try to block out his unhappy feelings.

Some people drink as an escape from having to face up to situations they feel unable to handle. Although alcohol may temporarily make a person forget his or her worries, the problem will still remain when the effects of the alcohol have worn off. Far from solving anything, using alcohol in this way can make a situation worse. Drinking alcohol does not make a problem go away.

When other people around you are drinking alcohol, you may feel pressure to drink, even if you don't want to.

Some people may make fun of others who do not drink, but drinking alcohol is a choice. Each person has the right not to do it. Drinking alcohol does not make you a better or more impressive person.

It is important to remember that the image of alcohol as presented in advertisements is often very different from the effect that alcohol can have in real life.

GETTING DRUNK

EVEN SMALL AMOUNTS OF ALCOHOL CAN HAVE A SIGNIFICANT EFFECT ON YOUR BODY AND BEHAVIOR, WHETHER YOU NOTICE IT OR NOT.

Drunkenness is actually a form of poisoning.
Getting drunk means drinking enough alcohol to severely affect your ability to function properly. In fact, the amount of alcohol which makes people drunk differs for everyone. It depends on the age, sex, size, and state of health of the person who is drinking. But even those who are similar in these respects may differ in their physical and emotional reactions to alcohol. The composition of women's bodies means that they will tend to become drunk more quickly than men. Many people forget how easy it is for drinking alcohol to get out of hand. Alcohol can alter moods and make people argumentative or very sentimental. It may affect people's co-ordination, making walking and talking difficult. It affects the ability to think clearly.

Being drunk is often seen as a bit of fun. Even people who know they have had enough will dare each other to have another drink. This can be dangerous, making you take risks you wouldn't otherwise take.

▽ Two weeks later, the Sharpes and Fishers went abroad on vacation.

THIS IS THE LIFE!

YES, IF YOU LIKE BEING BORED TO DEATH.

WHAT IS WRONG WITH YOU? YOU'VE DONE NOTHING BUT MOAN SINCE WE ARRIVED.

▽ Scott said he was missing his friends and there was nothing to do in the hotel.

THERE'S A DISCO FOR US TONIGHT. I'D LIKE TO GO.

THAT SOUNDS LIKE FUN. I DON'T SUPPOSE YOU WANT TO COME WITH US TO THE CABARET?

NO WAY. I SUPPOSE A DISCO COULD BE OK.

▽ That night, Scott, Ben, and Paige went to Marsha's parents' room before the disco.

YOU CAN'T DO THAT. MY DAD WILL NOTICE THERE'S SOME MISSING.

DON'T WORRY. YOU CAN'T HAVE A DISCO WITHOUT ALCOHOL. COME ON, GUYS. DON'T BE SUCH BABIES.

▽ At the disco, Marsha and Paige went to dance. Scott poured some whisky into Ben's glass.

IT TASTES STRANGE. IT'S BURNING MY THROAT.

DO YOU DRINK THIS STUFF A LOT?

SOMETIMES. SO WHAT? IT HELPS ME HAVE A GOOD TIME. WHAT'S THE BIG DEAL?

▽ An hour later, they had become friendly with some other young people.

THIS IS BETTER THAN I THOUGHT IT WOULD BE. HOW LONG ARE YOU HERE FOR?

ANOTHER WEEK. WHAT'S THIS?

IT'S JUST WINE. ANDY GOT IT FROM ROOM SERVICE. HE PRETENDED TO BE HIS DAD!

WE SHOULD GO SOON, SCOTT. I DON'T THINK MARSHA'S FEELING VERY WELL.

OK. THE DISCO CLOSES SOON, ANYWAY. LET'S GO TO THE POOL.

LOOK AT ANDY AND FIONA. THEY'RE DANCING REALLY CLOSE.

△ The four of them left soon afterward.

Getting Drunk

▽ Once outside, Scott started to fool around.

> SCOTT, GET DOWN FROM THERE. THAT'S DANGEROUS.

> I NEED TO GET BACK TO THE ROOM. I THINK I'M GOING TO BE SICK.

▽ They sneaked into Marsha's room, hoping her parents would be out.

> MARSHA'S NOT WELL. SHE MUST HAVE EATEN SOMETHING BAD.

> DRUNK SOMETHING MORE LIKE. LOOK AT YOU. WHAT HAVE YOU BEEN UP TO?

> WE'RE SORRY, MR. SHARPE. SOME OTHER KIDS HAD SOME BOOZE WITH THEM. WE THOUGHT IT WOULD BE OK.

▽ The adults came into the room. Mrs. Sharpe went to look after Marsha.

> ARE YOU SURE THEY WERE THE ONLY ONES WITH SOME ALCOHOL? MY WHISKY BOTTLE SEEMED RATHER EMPTY.

> I'VE WARNED YOU ABOUT THIS, SCOTT. YOU'RE TAKING AFTER YOUR DAD. YOU'RE STAYING WITH ME ALL DAY TOMORROW.

> WE ONLY TOOK A BIT. THIS HAS NOTHING TO DO WITH DAD. ANYHOW, YOU'RE ALL DRINKING. I'M SICK OF EVERYONE TREATING ME LIKE A CHILD.

▽ Scott stormed out. Mrs. Sharpe came out of the bathroom.

> MARSHA'S FINE. SHE'S BEEN REALLY SICK, BUT THAT'S PROBABLY FOR THE BEST. WE OBVIOUSLY CAN'T TRUST YOU ON YOUR OWN.

> WE'RE SORRY ABOUT TAKING THE WHISKY. WE DIDN'T MEAN IT. IT JUST GOT OUT OF HAND.

> SCOTT'S RIGHT, HOW COME IT'S OK FOR YOU ALL TO DRINK?

> WE'RE ALL ADULTS, AND WE'RE RESPONSIBLE ENOUGH NOT TO BE ROLLING ABOUT DRUNK.

> NO ONE SAID THERE WAS ANYTHING WRONG WITH HAVING A DRINK, BEN.

▽ The next day, Marsha had a hangover.

> I FEEL TERRIBLE. I'M NOT DOING THAT AGAIN. HOW ARE YOU? DID YOU GET INTO TROUBLE?

> I THOUGHT I'D NEVER HEAR THE END OF IT. I FEEL A BIT IFFY, TOO, AND SCOTT'S BEING IMPOSSIBLE. MOM'S TRIED TO TALK TO HIM, BUT HE JUST WON'T LISTEN.

> HE JUST WALKED OUT THIS MORNING, SAYING HE WAS GOING TO FIND ANDY AND FIONA. HE'S IN A REALLY STRANGE MOOD.

△ Mrs. Fisher sent Ben and Paige back to their room, and said she would be talking to them in the morning.

13

Marsha had a hangover the morning after she got drunk. A hangover is the after-effect of the poison of the alcohol on the body. It affects most people who drink a lot of alcohol. A hangover can cause headaches and feelings of nausea. It can also make people forget what happened when they were drunk and make it difficult for them to be fully alert for most of the day. There are lots of supposed cures for a hangover but in reality the only true cure is time – or to drink very little or not at all.

Andy and Fiona are dancing closely.

Many young people have found themselves in sexual situations or have been tempted to experiment with other drugs, because the alcohol has stopped them from making safe decisions. Alcohol muddles your judgment. Even if you are determined not to do something at the beginning of the evening, you may find yourself going along with things once you have had a few drinks. This can lead you into difficult and even dangerous situations.

Attitudes toward people who are drunk vary greatly.

Some people believe that being able to drink a large amount of alcohol is a sign of being mas- culine and is acceptable for men. They think that drinking a lot makes women "unfeminine." But being drunk is not attractive, whatever your sex.

ALCOHOL AND THE BODY

ALCOHOL IS ABSORBED INTO THE BODY VERY QUICKLY. WITHIN MINUTES OF A PERSON TAKING A DRINK, IT HAS REACHED THE BRAIN, MUSCLES, NERVES, AND OTHER PARTS OF THE BODY.

Alcohol is a depressant drug. It interferes with the body systems.
This means that it slows down the brain's responses, making reactions slow and muddling thought. As well as a loss of co-ordination, the effects that alcohol can have include vomiting and headaches.

Long-term abuse of alcohol can cause high blood pressure and serious damage to the liver, whose job it is to break down alcohol into less harmful substances. Alcohol can harm the heart, brain, and nervous system. A large amount of alcohol taken in a short period may cause people to slip into a coma, and can even prove fatal. Alcohol is very dangerous when taken at the same time as medicines or other drugs.

Research has suggested that some alcoholic drinks may actually be beneficial to adults, if taken in very small quantities. However, most people who drink alcohol exceed these safe limits very quickly.

These are some of the effects that drinking too much alcohol over a period of time can have on the body.

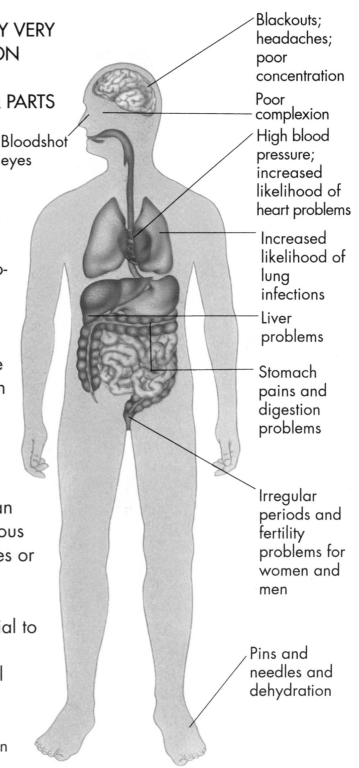

Bloodshot eyes

Blackouts; headaches; poor concentration

Poor complexion

High blood pressure; increased likelihood of heart problems

Increased likelihood of lung infections

Liver problems

Stomach pains and digestion problems

Irregular periods and fertility problems for women and men

Pins and needles and dehydration

▽ On their return from vacation, the Sharpes took Rachel and Laurence a present.

THANK YOU. IT'S OUR FAVORITE.

WE'LL PUT IT AWAY UNTIL AFTER THE BABY'S BORN. I'VE DECIDED NOT TO DRINK ANY ALCOHOL WHILE I'M PREGNANT, FOR THE BABY'S SAKE.

THAT'S VERY SENSIBLE, DARLING. I THINK THIS YOUNG LADY COULD DEFINITELY LEARN SOMETHING FROM THAT ATTITUDE.

▽ Marsha told Rachel about being drunk on vacation.

IT WAS SCOTT'S IDEA, BUT IT WAS MY OWN FAULT FOR GOING ALONG WITH HIM IN THE FIRST PLACE. I WAS A WRECK FOR TWO DAYS. IT CERTAINLY WASN'T HOW IT LOOKS IN THE ADVERTISEMENTS.

SHE COULD HARDLY LEAVE THE ROOM!

▽ Two weeks later, Jeff and Mehmet ran into Scott in town.

SCOTT WAS REALLY COOL TOWARD US AFTER THAT. HE'D GO OFF ON HIS OWN OR WITH ANDY AND FIONA. HE WAS SO MOODY. BEN AND PAIGE ARE REALLY WORRIED ABOUT HIM.

HI, SCOTT. WHAT ARE YOU UP TO? HOW WAS THE VACATION?

OK, I GUESS. I'M WAITING FOR JOHNNY. WHAT ARE YOU TWO DOING DOWN HERE?

YEAH, SORRY ABOUT THAT. I'VE BEEN KIND OF BUSY. YOU KNOW HOW IT IS.

I HARDLY EVER SEE YOU THESE DAYS. BUT I CAN SEE YOU'VE GOT SOME NEW FRIENDS.

WHAT'S THE MATTER WITH SCOTT? HE LOOKS A MESS.

WE'RE ON OUR WAY TO THE POOL. WHERE THE TWO OF US WERE SUPPOSED TO GO SWIMMING BEFORE YOU WENT ON VACATION. REMEMBER?

ARE YOU COMING, SCOTT? I'VE GOT THE STUFF.

HE'S REALLY CHANGED RECENTLY. WE'D ARRANGED ALL SORTS OF THINGS FOR THE HOLIDAYS, BUT HE JUST KEEPS MAKING EXCUSES.

△ Scott said he'd see Jeff around, and left with Johnny and his friends.

△ Jeff was worried that Scott would get into trouble if he wasn't careful.

Rachel knows it is important to avoid alcohol when pregnant because it can harm an unborn baby. Alcohol absorbed into the mother's blood passes to the growing baby. A baby born to a woman who is a heavy drinker may have physical and mental abnormalities. Doctors recommend that pregnant women should be very careful about the amount of alcohol they drink.

Jeff knows that people can become physically dependent upon alcohol. This means that their bodies become so used to the effect of alcohol that they seem to crave the alcohol. They may wake up shaking, and the only way they can think of stopping this is by taking another drink. In this way, they become more and more addicted to alcohol, both physically and emotionally.

Alcohol doesn't just affect the inside of the body. It can make a difference in your appearance as well. Alcoholic drinks contain none of the essential nutrients the body needs. They do, however, have a large amount of calories. This can lead to weight gain, affecting the whole body – not just a beer belly!

Alcohol may also make you look puffy and spoil your complexion, causing spots. It stimulates and enlarges the blood vessels, creating a flushed look.

However, people who continue to drink heavily may reach a point where they no longer care about the way they look or what they eat.

ALCOHOL AND BEHAVIOR

ALCOHOL CAN SIGNIFICANTLY AFFECT THE WAY A PERSON FEELS AND BEHAVES.

When people have drunk alcohol, they may not even realize that they are acting any differently.

Alcohol is an unpredictable drug. It can make people feel confident and in control, even though it is really clouding their abilities and judgment. People who have had

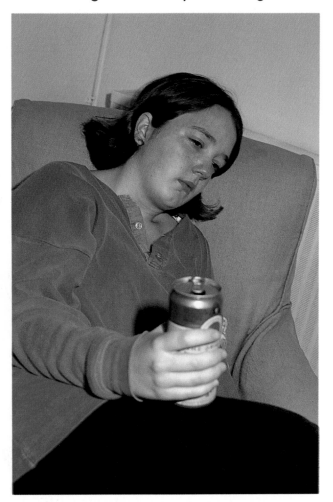

a drink have a greater chance of having accidents, because they are unable to judge situations carefully. They may also be persuaded into situations which they later regret.

Behavior may not always be consistent. Someone may be happy one moment but angry or violent the next. Some people start to speak very loudly and stop making sense, even though they do not realize this themselves. The effect of alcohol on a person's emotions and behavior often depends on how he or she was feeling beforehand. It can make people more depressed even though they may have drunk in order to feel good. But it can also make people miserable, even if they felt fine before drinking. Long-term alcohol abuse, or the effects of a hangover, may force people to take time off work.

People cannot control the effect that alcohol has on their feelings. It may often make them very tearful and emotional.

▽ A few weeks later, Scott told his mom he was ill and couldn't go to school.

THIS IS THE THIRD TIME SINCE SCHOOL STARTED THAT YOU'VE MISSED A DAY. I'M NOT STUPID, SCOTT, AND I'M TOO USED TO THE SIGNS TO KNOW THAT YOU'RE DRUNK, NOT ILL. WHY WON'T YOU TALK TO ME? I'M WORRIED ABOUT YOU.

I'M OK. LEAVE ME ALONE. I JUST DON'T FEEL WELL, THAT'S ALL.

MOM KEEPS JOKING ABOUT HOW MUCH ALL THE TAXIS ARE COSTING THEM.

I THOUGHT YOUR DAD DROVE.

HE DOES, BUT HE LOST HIS LICENSE LAST YEAR FOR DRUNK DRIVING.

△ Mr. Fisher had been banned from driving and had to pay a large fine.

▽ Marsha caught up with Ben and Paige on the way to school.

MOM TOLD ME YOUR MOM AND DAD MIGHT BE GETTING BACK TOGETHER. IS IT TRUE?

WE HOPE SO. NOTHING'S CERTAIN YET, THOUGH. THAT'S WHY WE HAVEN'T REALLY TOLD ANYONE.

IT'S GREAT HAVING DAD AROUND AGAIN. THEY DON'T WANT TO RUSH THINGS, THOUGH. THEY'VE JUST BEEN OUT A FEW TIMES - DAD GOT INTO QUITE A LOT OF DEBT WITH HIS DRINKING.

▽ That evening, Jeff met Scott in the street, with Johnny Christian. He could tell they had both been drinking.

I WENT TO YOUR HOUSE WHEN YOU DIDN'T COME TO SCHOOL. MR. DYTON WAS ASKING ABOUT YOU. YOU MISSED SWIM PRACTICE AGAIN.

WHO'S THIS, SCOTTY? HE SOUNDS LIKE YOUR MOTHER.

WHO CARES ABOUT SWIM PRACTICE? I'VE GOT MORE IMPORTANT THINGS TO DO.

LIKE WHAT? GETTING DRUNK? OH YEAH, THAT'S VERY CLEVER. YOU'LL GET INTO TROUBLE IF YOU GO ON LIKE THIS.

IF YOU DON'T GET OUT OF MY WAY, I'M GOING TO HURT YOU!

SERVES YOU RIGHT. I DIDN'T ASK FOR YOUR OPINION. I KNOW WHAT I'M DOING.

I THOUGHT WE WERE FRIENDS, BUT YOU'VE CHANGED SO MUCH.

△ Jeff tried to reason with him. Suddenly, Scott lashed out with his fist.

△ Scott left with Johnny. He was upset at having hit Jeff. He had never done anything like that before.

Scott has had a drink, lost his temper, and hit Jeff.

Many people involved in violent incidents have been drinking alcohol. Alcohol lowers a person's self control. Violence can be sparked off by a chance remark or for no apparent reason. This often happens with groups of people who have been drinking. Alcohol can also make people misjudge just how aggressive they are being.

By drinking and driving, Mr. Fisher put both himself and other drivers at serious risk.

Every year, people are killed or badly injured as a result of people driving while under the influence of alcohol. This is why many countries have strict laws about drinking and driving. Driving requires much skill and concentration, but drinking alcohol interferes with a driver's ability and judgment. Many people believe that drivers should not be allowed to drink any alcohol at all.

People can become emotionally dependent on alcohol.

Drinking can become so much a part of a person's life that he or she feels unable to do without alcohol. People may rely on it to help them to cope with all kinds of situations. They believe that if they stop drinking life won't be as much fun. If they began to drink to make themselves feel more confident in social situations, they may feel uncomfortable without an alcoholic drink. An emotional dependence on alcohol often means that a person is or will become physically addicted as well.

EFFECTS ON RELATIONSHIPS

AS WELL AS DAMAGING A PERSON'S HEALTH AND WELL-BEING, ALCOHOL CAN AFFECT RELATIONSHIPS WITH OTHER PEOPLE.

Relationships can suffer as a result of even just a few drinks.
People who have had an alcoholic drink may say things they don't mean and small arguments can be blown out of proportion. Someone who gets drunk regularly may become unreliable because alcohol can affect a person's memory. People who are dependent on alcohol will think of little else other than drinking. They may try to hide the problem. If you live with someone like this, you may feel no longer able to trust the person. Some people grow to feel ashamed of a person they still love very much. The family of someone with an alcohol problem will often have to cope with confusing and upsetting feelings.

Alcohol can make someone who is usually very quiet become suddenly violent. Or he or she may become unpredictable and neglect the people who are closest to them.

▽ The next evening after school Scott's teacher, Mr. Rogers, asked him to stay behind.

I'M VERY DISAPPOINTED IN YOUR WORK THIS SEMESTER, SCOTT. YOU'RE A BRIGHT BOY, BUT YOU DON'T SEEM TO CARE WHETHER YOU DO WELL OR NOT ANYMORE. IS THERE SOMETHING WRONG?

NO, EVERYTHING'S FINE.

WELL, SOMETHING'S THE MATTER. YOU'VE BEEN OUT OF SCHOOL A LOT, YOUR WORK'S SUFFERING, AND YOU'VE BEEN MISSING SWIM PRACTICE. SCOTT, IF THERE'S ANYTHING YOU WANT TO TALK ABOUT, YOU CAN ALWAYS COME TO ME.

△ Deep down, Scott did want to ask for help, but he was afraid to admit he had a problem.

▽ Scott said Johnny had thought the whole thing was just a joke.

▽ The next morning, Ben and Paige came into Scott's room.

JEFF WAS JUST ON THE PHONE. HE SAID YOU TWO HAD ARGUED. HE WANTED TO MAKE SURE YOU WERE ALL RIGHT.

DID HE TELL YOU I'D HIT HIM, TOO? I DIDN'T MEAN TO. I'D BEEN DRINKING AND I JUST FLIPPED. I DON'T REALLY UNDERSTAND WHAT'S HAPPENING.

HE AND HIS GIRLFRIEND GET SO AGGRESSIVE WHEN THEY'VE BEEN DRINKING. IT'S NOT AS IF JOHNNY'S PARENTS DRINK. IT'S FRIGHTENING WHAT ALCOHOL CAN MAKE YOU DO. I'VE EVEN BEEN STEALING FROM MOM TO PAY FOR IT.

I THOUGHT IT WOULD MAKE ME FEEL MORE CONFIDENT, BUT I JUST FEEL OUT OF CONTROL.

THAT'S WHAT DAD SAID. WHEN HE AND MOM ARGUED HE SAID TERRIBLE THINGS. HE DIDN'T MEAN THEM, BUT HE STILL SAID THEM.

YOU NEED TO GET SOME HELP, SCOTT. PLEASE TALK TO MOM AND DAD.

THEY'LL KNOW WHAT TO DO.

THEY'RE BOTH WORRIED ABOUT YOU.

△ Scott knew he needed to talk to someone.

GIVE ME A BIT OF TIME TO THINK. I FEEL LIKE I'VE LET THEM BOTH DOWN. YOU'D THINK I'D KNOW BETTER, ESPECIALLY BECAUSE OF DAD.

Every person needs to have a feeling of his or her own worth.

A drinking problem can severely affect a person's sense of their own value. They may lose interest in themselves and those around them. This may also affect friends or relatives of those with a problem. It can be upsetting if you are treated badly because of someone else's problem. But remember that it is not your fault – we are all responsible for our own behavior. If a situation is making you unhappy, it can help to talk to an adult whom you trust.

Young people may feel they have to cover up for the behavior of parents who drink a lot.
They may think there is nothing they can do about the problem but feel that they have to make excuses for the person concerned. They might also worry about what others will think if they find out. It can be hard to hear people saying unkind things about a person you love.

People who are drunk are often unable to think and talk sensibly.
Ben and Paige remember how worried they were because their parents argued all the time when their dad had been drinking. It can be very upsetting if someone is arguing when drunk. He or she will often not make very much sense.

ATTITUDES TOWARD ALCOHOL

IN MANY SOCIETIES, DRINKING ALCOHOL IS AN ACCEPTABLE CHOICE. HOWEVER, PEOPLE HAVE VERY DIFFERENT VIEWPOINTS ON THE SUBJECT.

Many believe that because alcohol is so widely used and available that there is a danger of forgetting the problems that it can cause. Those who try to make others aware of the risks, or who choose not to drink alcohol, are often seen as killjoys, because of the way people associate alcohol with a good time. Some organizations campaign for action to be taken against alcohol abuse and for stricter regulations regarding the consumption of alcohol, particularly in relation to drinking and driving.

Some drinks are advertised in a glamorous way. This often contrasts with the actual effect that drinking them has on people.

▽ A few days later, Scott told his parents everything.

I LIKED DOING IT, THAT'S THE THING. IT MADE ME FEEL GOOD AT THE TIME. I NEVER THOUGHT IT WOULD GET SO OUT OF HAND, EVEN THOUGH I KNEW WHAT YOU'D GONE THROUGH.

I KNOW SON. I USED TO THINK OF MYSELF AS A SOCIAL DRINKER. IT TOOK ME A LONG TIME TO REALIZE THAT THE ALCOHOL WAS CONTROLLING ME AND NOT THE OTHER WAY AROUND.

THE IMPORTANT THING IS THAT YOU'RE TALKING TO US, SCOTT.

▽ A couple of days later, after school, Johnny Christian came over to Scott.

HEY, SCOTTY, WHERE HAVE YOU BEEN HIDING? ARE YOU ON FOR TONIGHT? BRING SOME MONEY, I'LL GET THE BOOZE.

I'M SORRY, JOHNNY. I CAN'T HANDLE THIS ANYMORE. I'M GETTING INTO TROUBLE AT SCHOOL AND EVERYTHING.

I THOUGHT YOU WERE OK. BUT I SHOULD HAVE KNOWN, YOU'RE JUST DUMB. DON'T EXPECT ANY FAVORS FROM ME.

▷ Scott walked away, and went to find Jeff.

DON'T WORRY, I WON'T. SEE YOU AROUND.

I'M REALLY SORRY ABOUT WHAT HAPPENED BEFORE. I WAS OUT OF HAND.

YOU BET. LOOK, FORGET IT. I'M JUST GLAD YOU'RE OK.

△ Scott told him he was doing much better. He'd even persuaded Mr. Dyton to let him try out for the swim team again.

YOU SHOULD HAVE BEEN LIKE MEHMET. HE'S NOT ALLOWED TO DRINK ALCOHOL BECAUSE OF HIS RELIGION.

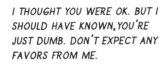

BUT THAT DOESN'T MEAN I WOULDN'T LIKE TO, SOMETIMES. ESPECIALLY WITH THE WAY THEY MAKE IT LOOK IN FILMS.

◁ Mehmet said that lots of his friends drank alcohol, even though they weren't supposed to.

▷ The next day, Ben and Paige were at Marsha's house.

I SAW JOHNNY CHRISTIAN LAST NIGHT. HE AND HIS FRIENDS WERE HANGING OUT BY THE SHOPPING MALL, FOOLING AROUND.

I'M GLAD SCOTT'S NOT PART OF THAT GROUP ANYMORE.

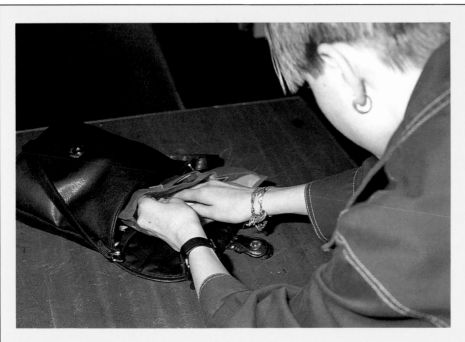

Alcohol is expensive to buy, as Scott knows.
People who are dependent on alcohol can run up huge debts, or even turn to stealing, to get the money they need to be able to buy it.

Governments earn a lot of money from taxes on alcohol. Businesses make millions from its manufacture. It is therefore likely to remain a legal drug in most societies for years to come. This is why it is important to know the effect it can have on your life if not used sensibly.

People in many social situations often drink alcohol automatically. They may describe themselves as a "social drinker," intending this to mean that they do not have a problem with alcohol. But this is not always the case. Often, social drinkers do not realize the amount of alcohol they are consuming. In fact, people who regularly drink heavily but call themselves social drinkers, may actually be alcoholic – dependent on the alcohol.

Some cultures and religions ban the drinking of alcohol.
Even so, if you live in a society or country where alcohol is accepted and available, but you have been told that you must not drink, it can sometimes be difficult to refuse. It can cause great upset and conflict if a member of a family whose culture or religion forbids the drinking of alcohol, chooses to drink. As Mehmet has said, the way in which alcohol is presented in the media can make it seem very tempting.

SENSIBLE DRINKING

ALCOHOL NEED NOT BECOME A PROBLEM FOR ANYONE IF PEOPLE UNDERSTAND THE RISKS AND DEVELOP A SENSIBLE ATTITUDE TOWARD IT.

Many young people are naturally curious about what drinking alcohol is like. Some will experiment and try it for themselves.
While one or two drinks are not likely to do any lasting damage, it is important to remember that young people can develop an addiction to alcohol just as easily as adults can. In addition, a young person's body may be undergoing many changes, especially during puberty. It is not helpful to put the extra demand on your body of having to break down the alcohol you have consumed.

Every person has the right to decide to drink or not to drink alcohol. The decision will depend on lots of factors, including your age, experience, and attitudes toward it. It is important not to be pressured into drinking just because other people think you should do it. In the same way, if you do eventually decide to drink alcohol, you should respect other people's decisions not to, and should not try to force them into doing something they don't want to do.

Alcohol plays a large part in many social occasions, but you always have the choice to say no to the offer of alcohol, at any time.

▽ It was two months later, close to Christmas. The Fishers were having a small party.

SCOTT SEEMS TO BE DOING WELL. YOU MUST BE GLAD HE CAME TO YOU FOR HELP.

I AM. I THOUGHT SOMETHING WAS WRONG BUT JUST KEPT TELLING MYSELF IT WAS ONLY A PHASE. THERE SEEMED TO BE SO MANY WORSE THINGS HE COULD HAVE BEEN DOING. I REALIZE NOW HOW STUPID THAT WAS. I SHOULD HAVE DONE SOMETHING SOONER.

YOU CAN'T BLAME YOURSELF. KIDS HAVE A RESPONSIBILITY FOR THEIR OWN LIVES, TOO. RACHEL WILL BE FINDING THAT OUT SOON!

SO, MEHMET, DID YOU SEE SCOTT IN THE SWIMMING FINALS?

YES I DID. YOU DID REALLY WELL, SCOTT. YOU TOO, JEFF.

NEXT TIME, I'LL WIN. I TRIED REALLY HARD, BUT I'D JUST MISSED TOO MUCH PRACTICE. IT TOOK A LONG TIME TO GET INTO SHAPE AGAIN.

△ Mr. Fisher went to get some food.

YOUR DAD SEEMS PROUD OF YOU.

IT MUST BE GOOD HAVING YOUR MOM AND DAD BACK TOGETHER AGAIN.

IT IS. WE'RE STILL WORKING THINGS OUT. IT'S LIKE GETTING TO KNOW EACH OTHER AGAIN. IT HASN'T BEEN EASY AND I CERTAINLY DIDN'T HELP.

HI, RACHEL. THE BABY'S DUE SOON, ISN'T IT? I THOUGHT YOU WEREN'T DRINKING UNTIL AFTER IT'S BORN.

THIS IS FOR LAURENCE. TO BE HONEST, I'VE BECOME SO USED TO NOT HAVING ALCOHOL, I DON'T MISS IT AT ALL. AT ONE TIME, I'D HAVE HAD A DRINK, JUST BECAUSE IT'S A PARTY.

YOU'RE LOOKING GOOD. HOW ARE THINGS?

FINE. I GO TO THIS GROUP FOR YOUNG PEOPLE WHO'VE ALL HAD PROBLEMS WITH ALCOHOL. TALKING ABOUT THINGS REALLY HELPS.

YOU'VE BEEN LUCKY, SCOTT. IT'S SO EASY FOR THINGS TO GET OUT OF HAND.

IT WASN'T ALL LUCK. THE POINT IS IT'S NEVER TOO LATE TO STOP. I KNOW THAT NOW. JOHNNY STILL BELIEVES HE DOESN'T HAVE A PROBLEM, BUT HE SHOULD TALK TO SOMEONE.

SCOTT RAN INTO JOHNNY THE OTHER DAY. HE'S STILL THE SAME.

MAYBE HE WILL EVENTUALLY. ALL THIS HAS MADE ME THINK ABOUT WHETHER I WANT TO DRINK ALCOHOL AT ALL WHEN I'M OLDER.

I THINK ALCOHOL'S OK IF YOU DON'T GO TOO FAR WITH IT. COME ON, LET'S GET SOMETHING TO EAT.

△ Scott said he'd tried to talk to Johnny, but Johnny wouldn't listen.

△ The four of them went to join the others.

People who decide to drink alcohol can take steps to avoid developing a problem.
Keeping track of the amount they are drinking is important, as is drinking slowly. Eating something when having alcohol or beforehand will slow down the rate at which alcohol is absorbed. Different kinds or strengths of alcohol should never be mixed. It is a good idea to alternate between an alcoholic and non-alcoholic drink.

Anyone arranging a party should make sure that there is a range of non-alcoholic drinks available. People should always feel free to refuse an alcoholic drink if they don't want one. Everyone who drinks alcohol should think carefully about the amount they consume.

Anyone who feels that they have an alcohol problem should not be afraid to ask for help, at any stage.
Scott knows that talking about his feelings earlier would have helped prevent the problem from becoming so serious. Now, he has started going to a group.

There are many counseling services and groups available all over the world. Many people with a serious problem will need to cut down on the amount they drink or give up alcohol altogether. This can be very difficult, but it can be done. People may need much encouragement from those close to them.

There are also many organizations which offer help and support to the family and friends of people who have a drinking problem.

WHAT CAN WE DO?

HAVING READ THIS BOOK, YOU WILL UNDERSTAND MORE ABOUT ALCOHOL AND THE EFFECTS IT CAN HAVE ON PEOPLE'S LIVES.

Alcohol is a drug. Although it is legal in most countries, like all drugs it can do serious damage if it is not used properly.
As you get older, you may be eager to try new things. But it is important to be aware of what experimenting might involve, and not to put yourself at risk. You know that alcohol does not make anybody more sophisticated or grown up. If you are already drinking alcohol, you need to think carefully about your reasons for doing so and the effect it might have on you and those close to you. Remember that it is never too late to seek help if you have a problem with alcohol.

Al-Anon Family Group Headquarters
P.O. Box 862,
Midtown Station
New York, NY 10018
(800) 356-9996

National Council on Alcohol and Drug Dependence
12 W. 21st Street
New York, NY 10010
(800) NCA-CALL

ADULTS CAN HELP TOO, BY REALIZING THAT THEIR ATTITUDE TOWARD
ALCOHOL CAN INFLUENCE THEIR CHILDREN'S VIEWS ABOUT DRINKING.

**If children see parents or relatives using alcohol freely, and perhaps
getting drunk, they may come to view this as acceptable behavior.**
Children and adults who have read this book together may find it useful to share
their thoughts and ideas about the issues raised. People who are experiencing
problems with alcohol might want to talk to someone who can
help. Information, advice, and support can be obtained
from the organizations listed below.

**Children of Alcoholics
Foundation**
P.O. Box 485,
Grand Central Station
New York, NY 10163-4185
(800) 359-COAF

Families Anonymous
P.O. Box 3475
Culver City,CA 90231-3475
(800) 736-9805

"Just Say No"
2101 Webster Street,
Suite 1300
Oakland, CA 94612
(800) 258-2766

**National Association for
Children of Alcoholics**
11426 Rockville Pike,
Suite 100
Rockville, MD 20852
(301) 468-0985

Alateen
1600 Corporate Landing
Parkway
Virginia Beach,
VA 23454-5617
(800) 356-9996

Alcoholics Anonymous
P.O. Box 459,
Grand Central Station
New York, NY 10163
(212) 870-3400

Target
11724 NW Plaza Circle
P.O. Box 20626
Kansas City, MO 64195
(800) 366-6667

**Allied Youth and Family
Counceling Center**
310 N. Windomere
Dallas, TX 75208
(214) 943-1044

INDEX

Photocredits
All the pictures in this book are by Roger Vlitos apart from pages: cover: Liz White; 3, 17 top, 20 bottom, 24, 26 bottom: Frank Spooner; 20 top: Rex.
The publishers wish to acknowledge that all of the photographs in this book have been posed by models.